# ODE TO STONE

Shirō Hara

Translated
with introduction
by
James R. Morita

East Asia Program
Cornell University
Ithaca, New York 14853

The *Cornell East Asia Papers* publishes manuscripts
on a wide variety of scholarly topics pertaining to
East Asia. Manuscripts are published on the basis
of camera-ready copy provided by the volume
author or editor.

Inquiries should be addressed to the Editorial
Board, East Asia Program, Cornell University,
140 Uris Hall, Ithaca, New York 14853.

# TABLE OF CONTENTS

## ACKNOWLEDGEMENTS

John Bennett of Columbus, Ohio, read a draft of my translation and offered me useful advice. Anonymous readers for Cornell University East Asia Papers gave me valuable criticisms. Michael Rake of the Computing Office of the College of Humanities, The Ohio State University, helped me to produce the final copy of the manuscript from the floppy disks of my personal computer. Shirô Hara encouraged my work, answering questions about words and interpretation. I am grateful to all of them.

The text I have used was *Chôhenshi: Ishi no fu*, published by Seidosha, Tokyo, in 1985.

# Translator's Introduction

Japanese poets seem no longer to believe that they can find beauty in traditional, ephemeral objects, such as flowers and birds, or that they can search for permanence in subtly changing seasons. Such times are considered long since passed. Having experienced a painful period of poetry of hopelessness and despair in the recent past, few now meditate in calmness to become one with nature again. Today, some claim that poetry is not an expression of emotion or intellect, and vigorously produce works even offensive to poetic sensitivity. They are challengers of the limits not only of language but vision and sound. Others detect spiritual barrenness and a deterioration of language, and insist on explication of ideology or feeling, while critics lament increasing isolation of the poets from the reader. However, the majority apparently think that they have exhausted all poetic resources, and continue to experiment with poetry by looking long and hard into what has not been explored by their predecessors.

In conditions such as this, some 5,000 "professional" poets can publish works in more than 1,000 competing poetry journals or numerous general magazines, while they produce some 600 individual collections of poems annually. With the unprecedented material prosperity of the country, there are prestigious and lucrative prizes given to Japanese poets. And this is concerned only with so-called *gendaishi*, or modern free verse, which was developed, as late as the end of the nineteenth century, by learning from European and American poetry. The contemporary popularity of traditional forms of poetry, the thirty-one syllable *tanka* and the seventeen syllable *haiku*, is an additional phenomenon. Many of these prospering Japanese poets, looking for more opportunities for experimentation and advancement, delve into subject matter remote from the realities of their present. Not only do they explore Greek and Japanese myths, but also such areas as Israeli

1

folklore, Indian legends, and the vanished Atlantis, and produce complex imagery in their search for new grounds in universality and permanent value. Some recent works are inevitably long--in fact, much longer than the ancient Japanese long poems, *chôka*, that fell into disuse after being championed by the early eighth century poet, Hitomaro.

The *Ode to Stone* is a long *gendaishi* translated from the Japanese of Shirô Hara (b. 1924), who has traveled throughout the world and sojourned twice in France. It was originally published as *Ishi no fu* in Tokyo in 1985, and awarded the *Gendai Shijin Shô*, a prize given annually by the Japan Modern Poets Association for an outstanding book of verse. Perhaps not coincidentally, one of the runners-up for the prize was also a long *gendaishi*. One critic called *Ode to Stone* an "epic" comparable to the great works produced in the twentieth century West. He referred not only to the poem's length but also to its epic quality of narrating the history of a people and their civilization.

Of course, neither "epic" nor "ode" is indigenous to Japanese poetry. The word *fu* in the original title, translated as "ode," is Chinese in origin and used in Japan to refer to certain Chinese poems composed by the Japanese in pre-modern days and to certain Japanese poems written today. Varying in its definition and being different from the Chinese originals of some two millennia ago, the Japanese *fu* is commonly a long poem which is free in form but well wrought, often classical in diction or tone, and depictive of emotions and thoughts. Some *fu* contain prose introductions and dialogues.

However, the original *Ishi no fu*, or "Ode to Stone," might very well have meant "ode on stone," "ode by stone," "stone's song," or even "rock's singing." In it, not a single first person pronoun is used, whether one reflective of the poet, as it was usually the case of the innumerable lyrical poems, or a fictive persona, as in much modern prose and verse. The fact that the subtitle to the poet's Afterword is "a personal expression" indicates that the author was conscious of the poetic stance he had established in the work as well as the prevailing criticism of the personal expressions that many Japanese writers make in their works.

Then again, the "personal expression" at the end of *Ode to Stone* may well be fictive.

In this work, stone is the assumed narrator. Like the epic hero in a nomadic tradition that Japan lacks, stone appears in Paris, in Cairo, in the twentieth century, in a historical past and in the future, and in various forms and styles. It is possible to consider that Hara is comparing the variety of stone to that of language: each stone, with its own silent history, enables the poet to calmly exercise his language to its limits. By pursuing stone, the poet pursues language.

The *Ode to Stone* is constructed in such a way that stone outside of Japan appears in its odd numbered sections, and stone in Japan, in the even numbered ones. This is a rather simple structure, as compared with more complex long *gendaishi*, many of which are installed in magazines sporadically, as though each installment were an independent piece. When such pieces are put together as a book, they are called *renshi* (linked modern poems), an obvious derivative of the medieval *renga* (linked verse) or *renku* (linked haiku). The linking techniques of such poems appear arbitrary and puzzling to the reader. In *Ishi no fu*, stone straightforwardly narrates Paris' cobblestone, Amsterdam's bridges, Lisbon's aqueducts, Ireland's forts, Egypt's pyramids, China's Great Wall, and other stone. However, it is an old stone bridge in Nagasaki, Hara's hometown, that prevails throughout the poem. Fondly called Eyeglasses Bridge because of its double-arched shape, it has endured the test of time. The Bridge is a symbol of permanence, the standard against which to judge all structures, whether of stone or of language.

The Bridge is sturdy because it possesses the ability to move according to changing conditions. It was built by Great-great-grandfather, the ancestral Japanese, using a secret method of building a stone structure on a soft foundation. That method was a result of the unification of Western and Japanese wisdom and technology during the sixteenth century. However, because of its very sturdiness, the Bridge became a dam at times of flooding and caused more damage to the town and its people than other bridges that broke away. What is the significance of being strong to the point of "permanence"? But what is permanence, the poet asks.

Here there is a reference to the seventeenth century master poet Bashô, whose cardinal principle it was to equate change to permanence. *Ode to Stone* examines the dichotomy of permanence and change, so to speak, or concreteness and abstraction, concentration and dispersion-- stone's substance--while encompassing both the beneficial and damaging, the upside and downside, the solid and elastic, and other extremities. Its technique is mature, digesting the previous experiments by the avant-garde poets. The result is a rather modest, long *gendaishi*. Unlike other contemporary long poems, it quietly appeals to common sense as well as poetic sensitivity.

Yet, the poet cannot help being critical of politics and the human foibles that result from it. Politicians dispute over the stone bridge's safety and replace it with a steel bridge. The bridge is reconstructed in a park, and the government designates it as a "permanent" cultural property. It is dead stone, however, for it lacks the weight of people who cross it, let alone the movable foundation to sustain its own weight. The poet recalls, with abhorrence, Antonio Gaudí's "art" park, and contemplates the greatness of Bashô who, sleeping with a stone as pillow on the roadside, established the lasting poetic. The poem evolves around these structures, involving the ancestors who built them, the warriors who fought and died by them, the townspeople who appreciated them, and the politicians who rebuilt them, seeking permanence in the world, in a hometown and in the poet himself.

Despite the stone's conscious attempt not to use a first person pronoun in the work, *Ode to Stone* autobiographically immortalizes the author. Hara grew up in Nagasaki, observing the Eyeglasses Bridge. Nagasaki was the Designated Treaty Port, though which the Japanese absorbed the Western civilization during the pre-modern era of the country's isolation policy. In those days, intellectuals gathered there, studied Dutch books, and advanced their knowledge. Hara went to Tokyo, and studied Japanese literature and stylistics. He published collections of his poems, *Fûryû ni tsuite* (On Refinement, 1963),

*Yûreitachi* (Ghosts, 1977), and *Aisatsu* (Greeting, 1980). Rarely loquacious, he writes, avoiding abstraction. In contrast to his contemporaries who, relying on music, theater, and the like, produce loud, incantational effects in reciting their works, Hara assiduously piles his language, so to speak, and creates a structure of discursive meaning. Obviously, he does not challenge, but rather cherishes his own limits of language. This poet is still concerned with what poetry means as well as how that meaning comes about.

That is what he means by *style*. Style is not what is now fashionable, unusual, or abstruse. It can be old, unnoticeable, and indistinguishable, but on its underside it is refined, quietly emitting a gleam. It is like the Paris street worker's skill of laying stone or the Nagasaki laborer's precision in piling stone blocks on soft soil. It is something aged, yet tenuous and quite vital, governed by the power of permanence at each of its moments of change. That style is endangered like the vanishing stone artisans who make meager living in the back streets of today's world.

Like most other contemporary Japanese poets, Hara has a good full-time job. He teaches modern Japanese literature at his alma mater, Waseda University, in Tokyo. He has published studies on stylistics and modern Japanese poets, while also enjoying journalistic popularity as an essayist and calligrapher. In addition, he is an avid rider of powerful motorcycles and fast German cars. However, once asked by a reporter what he does best, he proclaimed that his specialty is to read the underside of language.

*Ode to Stone* is Hara's poetics. Stone seems finally equated to language. The most durable language, Hara says, is poetic, like the Eyeglasses Bridge that possesses an astonishing underside.

James R. Morita
Columbus, Ohio

ODE TO STONE

# ODE TO STONE

## I.  Two Stonemasons' Tale

Rue de Faubourg St. Antoine
is a street for furniture makers
big and small, with workshops
in the nooks and alleys on both sides
Drafters, carpenters, wood carvers
quilt men, tailors, fixture men, paint men
masons, uphosterers, and repairmen
They all are fine *Faubourgiens*
in the Faubourg district outside the old walls

Monsieur Brunet the stonemason
is in a back alley by Versaille
At age 60 he is the owner
of a shop that has its own sign
One of the vanishing artisans
actually a fine sculptor
he is robust
and he chisels marble every day
to make one table leg a week
or only one table in a whole month
for when not in the mood he kills half a day in a cafe
Moreover, he recently made a Japanese friend
with whom he drinks
His wife, far from displeased
comes along with Brunet
and says innocently let's go
like we're all going to work . . .
She's not talking about another cafe
we are going to a movie

--There's a terrific film at the Bastille
it's a story of chivalry
Our Joan of Arc, though having passed her prime
reveals her opulent bosom as she stands

--I think you're wrong
to talk about anything in terms of whether it's abstract
　　　　　or concrete
You just make something and that's all
or, something must be made, not to
make a living
(though that's the case sometimes)
but because things are necessary for living
I don't understand difficult things
but when you say abstraction, you are making
something concrete by abstraction
That's a roundabout logic
for example, a table I make is abstract
if you like abstraction so much
don't make anything
and keep thinking in your head
that's true abstraction
Making things
is a concrete act

Museums?
I don't go to such places
except when I was young
I went to see Michelangelo and da Vinci
in Italy marble statues had hands-off signs
but I touched every one of them anyway
How can you know the warmth of the stone
without ever touching it?

But you are certainly a *curiosité*
coming to my shop so often
like you are my *surveillant*
and you showed me wonderful pictures
stone images of Buddha on Japanese roadsides
Those *Jizô*!
Fantastically beautiful, I love them all
I want to see them with my own eyes
Totally different from antique store Buddhas
they are simple yet dignified
all with innocent faces like *bebés*
I especially like their anonymity
which is exactly my ideal
so let's have one more drink
You see, I am a simple stone table maker
I have never made those gaudy stone figures
that crowd the cemetery at Père Lachaise
vulgar depictions of crying or laughing men, no
I haven't, even though I was asked
I just build tables that endure abuse
with legs like those old candleholders on the wall
you once called "*pieds de chat*"
You say that's an old Japanese name?
Whatever, let's suppose they are *pieds de chat*
details don't matter
to create the feeling of a cat standing there softly
*Jizô*! that is *tiédeur*
I must get back to work now

Rue de Faubourge St. Antoine
is paved with stone
from Bastille to Nation

and retains the air of the Roman Empire's
    thoroughfare
It's very old
in the very old district of Maraise
where sixteenth and seventeenth century
    buildings stand
How beautiful stone is
(in the subway tunnel at Bastille
  is the foundation of the old prison made of stone)
(from the streets of Paris
  stone pavement is disappearing
  replaced by tar)
(in the University District on the Left Bank
  stone was pried up and thrown at the police
  and was replaced by asphalt
  Twenty years have passed since then)
Today cars and dump trucks run incessantly
toward St. Antoine Hospital
the University Hospital next to it
ambulances siren full speed
it's like every ambulance in Paris is there
Stone is being abused by the enormous traffic

--Cobblestone is a remnant of old buggy roads
Monsieur Allado says mumbling
He is a pavement repairman
laying stone with two helpers
in summer or winter
How they work is--
they mark the area where bumps are
(usually near an intersection)
by putting posts
stretch red and white off-limit ribbons

Remove stone on the surface
forming mounds of gravel
dig sand at the bottom
Yellowish earth of the European continent is shown
and 20 centimeters of brown soil is removed
More mounds are made
These steps take one whole day, depending
      on the area's size
and the next day new gravel and sand arrive
to replace the old
At this phase Allado begins his work
assistants spread new soil
put dry sand and level it
Allado lays stone from a corner
checking it with his eye and fingers
He balances himself in Chaplin shoe
bends his slim body of 180 centimeters
(How could the coarse stone manifest nature?)
Allado continues to lay stone one by one
the *tôfu*-shaped granite
weighing one to two kilos
(some might weigh three kilos)
Laid vertically like *tôfu*
each stone does look small
(But how could the pale-faced, feeble students throw
  these blocks, which are really heavy
  at de Gaulle's police during the riot?
  Probably they could not
  Stone couldn't have gone more than five meters
  it only injured the comrades
  Was it not that they only pried up the pavement
  to build some barricades of stone
  to block the armoured vehicles of the police?)

Allado has already laid about 30 blocks of stone
(in 30 minutes, at the speed of one per minute)
Laying them at right angles would be easier
from Bastille to Nation
then from Bastille to Bastille
toward both Squares like waves
or like fireworks exploding
blocks of stone are radially laid
Though each stone is square
small gaps between blocks create the waves
That's where Allado applies his skills
laying stone
two assistants spread sand
sweep with brooms
and the gaps are filled
sand is spread again
large shoes stomp
in a quick easy tempo
and the procedure comes to an end
This man Allado was treated to beer at a nearby cafe
by a Japanese who watched his work
Allado introduced himself
Egyptian, immigrant, age 53, and single

Allado talks little about his work
A complete opposite of Brunet
looking like an accomplished elder
he is no ordinary eccentric
(It was about 8 P.M. one Friday, summer, the sun
        still high)
Allado dined with the Japanese man
he was unusually talkative
a bit drunk

--Cobblestone is a leftover from the buggy days
things change
(That was all he said about his work)
He talked instead about himself
--I was a stonecutter at Cairo
not a really good one
but of old stock
since the Age of Pyramids, my grandfather said
though he must have been exaggerating
I got married at 18
to a bride of 14
I truly loved her
but as soon as she got a taste of man
she began fooling around
with the stonecutters' union men
one after another
a bitch
unfaithful to me all the time
I knew
right after she slept with me
she went to another man
using up our money
she came to my workshop and demanded
          100 Egyptian pounds
she said her mother was sick
I knew she was lying
but I borrowed money and gave it to her
which she gave to another man
she kept on like that
so I got disgusted and divorced her
I've been a bachelor since then
I came to Paris
She's probably still in Cairo I don't know . . .

Allado talked as slowly
as the summer's day ended in Europe
But finally he got excited
and under his breath uttered
--Whore!
as though he had just discovered his wife's cheating
an event of some twenty years ago

To hear such a mundane story
from the lips of an obscure laborer
this close-mouthed stonemason from a land of
strict moral codes
is really very dear to my heart
(Every man in the world has some story in his life
  just as a hundred million men own at least
  three hundred million pairs of underpants)
But that has no connection with laid stone
neither man's grief nor joy affects stone
To think of stone in human terms
(such as whether stone will shine or sharpen
          according to man's emotion)
is man's conceit, romanticism, personification
Should stone be thought of in human terms
stone will demand a certain form
it will refuse to be set down
and want to be replaced by more compliant stone
(some stone may volunteer to be set in)
The stone layer obeys stone
listens to stone
that is all
There is only pure will
when stone and man become one

(Strategy in *go*
  is said to reflect the player's disposition
  but the stone on the game board
  is just a sign
  irrelevant to the stone in the pavement)
If the pavement reflects the layer's conditions
and reveals crookedness or gap
the pattern it forms might be interesting
but cars will destroy it in no time
To withstand weight
a simple law applies
Once man's desire or emotion intervenes
the road will no longer be road
The simple law is
that weight must be borne evenly
for stone to fight the pressures
that stone bounces back from below like springs
(if cars jolt, stone jolts)
If one stone butts out
all the stones lose balance
and the whole road will be bumpy in a day
These are the dynamics of democracy

September rain does not end
October is rainy
and the pavement stone glitters cold
florist's windows are steamed
Passing in a splashing ambulance
the dead of that evening are moving
toward the river
Are they returning to the 20th District
crossing the Seine?

A car is transporting a casket
which the impoverished immigrants
carried out the back entrance of the University
        Hospital
A Turkish hat
and a tiny wreath on the casket
Raindrops glisten on the black hat
Rain falls continually
and the Seine is swollen

## II.  Eyeglasses Bridge

Rain has been falling since the previous night
becoming harder at dawn
Warning bells fade
and roaring now like waterfalls
the siren is dopplerized
Evacuate, evacuate--voices too are vanishing
The river bank has collapsed
and the water is far above it
Where on earth do they want us to go
the front yard is like the sea
deeper than an adult's waist
driftwood runs like torpedos
furniture comes bobbing
then houses along the river start drifting
and people are swept into the torrent
The water keeps rising
it's beginning to cover tops of houses
Cries for help echo from the roofs
some brave the torrent only to be washed away
Children, cats, dogs, pigs, cows, women, men,
            carriages, and horses
are sinking in water
They can cry no more
those on the roof go where the roof goes
Atop a two-story house there are refugees
but the house melts
like a sugar cube in coffee

The other side of the town is like a dam
something is blocking the water
At the dam's edge
houses and furniture pile up
The people in the water
swiftly fall off the ends of the dam
Some go over the edge
down the deep muddy falls
like human trout

539 dead or missing
as reported on the international wire
Japan's worst flood
on July 25, 1957
rainfall 950 mm, i.e., 125 mm per hour
which may not look like much but the figures
were meaningless to the houses along the riverbank
everything was destroyed, even the foundations
The upper stream was worse
the water rose suddenly and receded quickly
into the sea--
carrying men with it
But what caused that dam?
It was the Eyeglasses Bridge
built in the nineteenth century
spanning the river 4 meters high
50 meters long
5.5 meters wide
with a big noselike girder in the middle
The arched stone bridge like a pair of eye glasses
became a weir for driftwood, houses, and walls
and stopped the enormous torrent

while many modern bridges of concrete and iron
were washed away
The stone bridge which used no concrete and which
       had never been reinforced
did not even shake
and sustained only minor damage
to the steps and railing
near the roads on both banks
The bridge withstood many floods


The Eyeglasses Bridge spans the Hommei River
that flows into the Sea of Ariake
25 kilometers N. E. of Nagasaki, Japan
in the town of Isahaya between Ômura Bay and Ariake


If only the Eyeglasses Bridge had not been there!
The Double-Arch Bridge doubled the damage!
townspeople remarked
(Man seeks to fault what's nearest him
  when heaven is too wide for blame)
Bloated bodies fill the lower stream
people culled the beach for more
The setting sun of July shone on the sea
and the wet gray sand stretched in the distance
The reeds by the embankment glisten
countless crab holes flicker ominously
the eyes of the dead are staring at the sky
Superior is the bridge of stone
the Eyeglasses Bridge killed men
(Here again, tragedy's depiction is personified
  the bridge cannot be blamed
  the bridge was just there)

Man hopes the dead will return on the tide
and watches the sea with water-soaked binoculars

Behind him is the muddy ruined town
with the stone bridge looming taller
The giant rims of the gray-colored Eyeglasses!

## III.  Sea Travel

*After the boat finally left the port to sea*
*I thought the pier's white stone was swollen*
wrote a student-soldier, who was killed in the war
Whether the sky was clear that day
water blue
mountains green
cheering voices present at the pier
the student-soldier did not record
he only noticed the whiteness of stone
What is certain however
is the fact that he never returned
He must have repeated good-bye
and the stone wall welled in his pupils
Dazzled by the glittering light
he moved his eyes
and the white wall fell with a tear

(Long ago, in the sixteenth century
  a young man traveled from Nagasaki, Japan
  to Europe on a Dutch ship
  his hair knotted and with a Japanese sword
  His mission was to learn how to build bridges)
((now a great-great-grandson of the ancestral father
        follows suit
  on a Polish freighter
  to get out of Japan
  Mingled with his own experience, the student-soldier's
  and the great-great-grandfather's))

The boat runs at the maximum allowable speed
full speed consumes too much fuel
and is not economical
What's important is being constant
the boat travels south in the East China Sea
three days after leaving Japan
the wind subsides
(the troopships go out of sight one by one)
and no sound of planes or anti-aircraft guns can be heard
not even a voice, only silence
Occasionally large seagulls appear
and perch silently on the mast
Three passengers of the boat
a German ex-sailor, an American youth
and a middle-aged Japanese who obviously has a past
follow the great-great-grandfather who rode a Dutch ship
Eating Polish sausage and hard brown bread
(which are so much better than the porridge on the
        troopship!)
looking into charts eagerly
great-great-grandfather's clumsy poem comes to mind
    *The sun in the South falls quickly*
    *With a thud, behind the dark clouds of Viet Nam*
A week after leaving Japan, at dawn in Singapore
a rustling noise of birds' feathers, seagulls
playing with white lace; like
the waves, over which travelers go
in search of distant stone
Maybe around here the great-great-grandfather wrote
      in Chinese
at his desk in the cabin after breakfast

*The ship, on a slate; the sea calm*
*Beyond, a constellation: the Southern Cross*
for the letter to mail in Singapore . . .
  Ominous noise
  of flying seagulls
  fills the sky
  Could the gulls be the spirits
  of those who died in anguish?
is the clumsy poem by his great-great-grandson
(Great-great-grandfather could not have written it
  at this site of a bloody battle fought only 40 years ago)


O young men who had no proper place to die!


(Stop indulging in recollection
  sentimentality is like sea sickness
  it only depresses man)
This is the time to move forward
or to return to great-great-grandfather's time
His sea travel
was filled with dreams and hopes
(and probably a bit of anxiety)
Observing the horizon day after day
he thought of the water's depth
marked the chart with an ink brush
valleys and gorges
and a prairie
connected to a plateau
He imagined the ship was flying above the sea's bottom
(Drain all water to the stratosphere, then the land
  will be mountains or a plateau or wilderness
  and peninsulas and capes will be mountain ridges
  Mountains will be mountains of the mountains)

Did the old chart indicate the water's depth?
(if it did, it must have been guess work)
On the bridge of the ship today
the chart clearly marking the water's depth
the ship enters the Andaman Sea
passes Ten-degree Strait
where water deepens from 200 meters
through a sharp incline
to 2,000, 3,000, and 4,000 meters
The trench where bubbles rise, pit and green reef
an unexplored sea
where fish and stones dance
The great virgin forest of water flowers
great-great-grandfather's sounding aparatus moved
        through
slowly at less than 10 knots per hour
Great-great-grandfather dreamed of Cairo
the Suez Canal was yet to be built
Above the great plateau 20,000 meters deep in the sea
the ship sailed south through the Indian Ocean
trying to reach the Cape of Good Hope
Today his great-great-grandson can bypass the Cape
travel north via the Red Sea, a way the great-great-
        grandfather couldn't even dream of
(the Red Sea is 2,000 meters deep)
Viewing Thebes on the left
he is about to complete the journey to Cairo

The sailors of the socialist country
are having a sumptuous Sunday breakfast
It's Easter
the Captain gave a talk yesterday

warning against rejecting Marxism as the
      eternal truth
Today wine is served
Marx is perhaps in heaven just for the day
Carrying big candy boxes in their hands
sailors retire to their cabins
Soon hesitantly
choruses of Christian hymns leak out
muffled voices of prayer
What wishes do you have
confused souls
Polish friends

## IV.   Cicadas' voice

Prayers continue
cicadas cry in unison
some 500 new epitaphs and urns line the altar
> *The true form of the stone bridge is not affected*
> > *by water or fire*
> *Immovable and lasting from beginning to eternity*
> *Yet merciless water wipes off months and years*
> *And man's life is like yesterday's dream . . .*

Guided to Nirvana are not those who are dead
but those who are sobbing
Priests in colorful costumes of all denominations
sit in the incense smoke
They are the descendants of Great-great-grandfather
who at the beginning of the nineteenth century
roamed villages in beggar's attire
in order to raise funds

Every time there was a flood
wooden bridges were lost
and of course houses and lives
(hence the place name Nagaremachi, a washedout town)
After the floods and suffering
the townspeople wanted an indestructible stone bridge
a long unfulfilled wish
because the town lacked funds
so the landlords and the rich men
even the poor saved on their food
and contributed to the priests
to build a stone bridge that could not be washed away

They had heard that western technology would enable
them to build such a bridge
with large *tatami*-size stone

Great-great-grandsons of those priests are offering prayers
for those "murdered" (so it is commonly said) by the
    indestructible stone bridge
Sobbing family members of the dead
are the great-great-grandchildren of the people
who gave gifts and labor
and the dead included many babies and children who
    could not swim
the children of the great-great-grandchildren

But why on earth did those new bridges
of steel and iron wash away
and the stone bridge that used no cement survive?
The townspeople were also puzzled about
why it served as a deadly dam
thinking of the spirits
of those whose graves are under the bridge
Townspeople had been told
that the bridge would never break because there
    are spirits
The belief became reality

The Eyeglasses Bridge must be removed
or it will become a dam again
only to cause more damage
People talked about this cultural property
and the city council fell into discord

This summer cicadas cry in unison

## V. Pyramid

Through hot desert
more than 200 kilometers diagonally from Suez
      to Nile
the route Great-great-grandfather probably took
wearing a sleeveless Japanese vest of hemp
a Japanese car runs
at 200 kilometers per hour
(a tankful of gas cost less than $6 for 40 litres in Suez
  roughly 35 yen a litre, only a quarter
  of the Japanese price)
(all of this would be inconceivable
  if it were in great-great-grandfathers' times
  but no matter
  now wanting to see the pyramid
  as he did
  as soon as possible and with as many views as possible
  and to return to the ship tomorrow
  Speed like Great-great-grandfather's
  will completely dehydrate a person
  No matter how much water you drink
  you only urinate once all day)
Sand surrounds the city
and the car goes through the maze of Cairo
(bypassing the Egyptian Museum)
the car crosses Tahrir Bridge on the Nile
and reaches the left bank

O golden, Great-great-grandfather's dream
appears so close on the sand slope over sand

(this side of the Qattara Depression)
casting a dark shadow against the setting sun

the PYRAMID!

Slabs of stone are being piled
each weighing 2.5 tons, five people haul one
Stonemasons, more numerous than the slabs
are silhouettes in the rays of the setting sun
On the slope leading to it is a line
of slaves voiceless like ants
rolling logs, pulling ropes, only the sounds of whips
are heard
The sand, the slabs, and the slaves
all in the gleam of rusty red

The stone ridges run east and west, north and south
over 100 meters high
each base extending more than 200 meters
What on earth is the meaning
of these 86 huge, geometric piles of stone?
Graves of the kings and queens who hold hands
in prayer
a guidebook says
100,000 people for 20 years
and some 2,300,000 slabs for one pile!
Was Great-great-grandfather really impressed
by this mass of power so incredibly large?
Simple appreciation is fine
even appropriate for such enormous objects
(look, for example, the Great Wall
Shih-fung-ti is said to have used several hundred
thousand slaves)

Travelers come visit ghosts' ruins
castles and other structures with maps in hand
match them against the registered names
and look around for marks through magnifying glasses
lavishly spend saved-up money
take notes
on the supremacy of power and its defiance of time
A universal pattern of seeing
attraction more appealing than nature itself
as though intrigues, violence, murders and such
are more appreciative than women or ripe tomatoes
Or maybe that's the very nature of semiotics
No one really sees stone
nor does anyone notice the slaves treading shadows
Travelers photograph the marks and go home
Such a simple way of recording emotions!

Chipped slates on the ground
(the facing of the pyramid has been stripped off
  perhaps stolen by people
  who used the pieces for their own houses
  that's some relief if true
  for it means they chipped away at power
  and the majestic pyramid is a stripped ruins
  the people made use of the surface slabs!)
Children are seen moving in and out like mice
at the air ducts 50 meters high
Slender men approach the travelers
innocent consumers (producers?) of the marks
and offer them camel rides
old women try to sell dubious ointments

boys on donkey's backs beg for pennies
a big adult is overjoyed given a ballpoint pen
These are the descendants of the stonemasons
      and slaves
living like sand on the expanse of sand

The sun sinks beyond the Qattara Depression
Great-great-grandfather!  Thebes is still far
600 kilometers upstream
Let these forms of power rest in this royal valley

## VI.  Dismantling

Dusk
it's time for stonemasons and their helpers to go home
the dismantling of the Eyeglasses Bridge has begun
with its cosmetic facing removed
the Eyeglasses Bridge is bare, and looks like it's
       being assembled

Under the bridge's arch
sturdy wooden scaffolds are built
to remove surface slabs from the railing
carefully one by one
the facing on the arch itself is pried up
The girder will be taken care of last
as planned and directed by Yûzô Yamaguchi
The veteran engineer had not worked with stone bridges
but no one else had qualifications
for dismantling, moving and rebuilding the bridge
More important he had a desire to find out
how on earth during the great-great-grandfathers' times
when foot messengers, palanquins, and sailboats were
       in use
when there was no cement
could they build a stone bridge of this size
gathering forces and funds
to satisfy people's needs, not for the politicians
How was it possible for them to build
the kind of bridge that outlasted modern bridges?

what formulas were applied to this beautiful bridge?
these were the questions Yûzô Yamaguchi asked
A hometown boy, quietly burning with passion
he was a fine engineer

No matter how beautiful the bridge is
times have changed
it destroyed lives, houses, property, and merchandise
so the bridge must go
The victims' relatives spoke up
and merchants supported the idea
even after a decision was made to move and restore it
      in a park
the opposition was strong
and proposed a housing project for the victims' relatives
Finally the proposal was tabled
and Yûzô Yamaguchi shouldered
both dismantling and restoration
He was devoted to the work, forgetting to eat

Each block of stone was numbered
wrapped in cloth, wrapped again in mat
and carefully laid on a truck bed with new carpet
(in one layer only, to avoid damage)

  Make way, these are precious stones!
  I wish I had a mat like that to sleep on
  You mean you want to sleep with stone?
  No, stone is too heavy for me!
Laborers talked loudly
(Were great-great-grandfathers like them?)

No such voices are heard now, and a chilly March
      night deepens
Yamaguchi alone is on the bridge
intently checking the measurement under a light
His trained eye does not miss the slightest gap
      in the stone

The dismantling continued
and surprises followed
No cement was found of course
but not even a scaffold had been used by the great-
      great-grandfathers
nor posts nor boards
let alone jacks
How on earth was the double-arch of stone blocks made?
They first built a sandbag hill
and climbed it with stone on their shoulders
(this was determined by the arch's curve)

What a simple method of construction
yet the stone blocks were connected together
making dismantling difficult
It wasn't just that the stone was laid tightly
but also deep beneath the surface
holes were drilled
and thick, short iron posts were stuck
A simple, yet solid principle of stone's union
the secret of iron ties!
This must be what Great-great-grandfather learned
      in Europe
and handed down to great-grandfathers
Great-great-grandchildren and their children
      had thought

that the Eyeglasses Bridge was sturdy because
    of the stone's weight
but they were proven wrong
The principle of stone's union is
that stone supports stone
where weight becomes insignificant
Gravity is cancelled out
In addition to iron ties
stone was cut in L-shape
and was engaged with other slabs
the same old technique found in stone buildings
    in Europe
and in marble sculptures
(especially for arms and legs)
also in Japanese carpenters' work
to join two wood pieces
(Coincidence of Western and Eastern wisdoms!)
which also helped maintain order
dispersion of weight
and the piled stone blocks never bulged
against the pressure from above
This simple but effective device
man prudently applied to stone's nature
Yet it's invisible from the stones' surface
showing only layers of stone
This beguiling aestheticism!

Yûzô Yamaguchi was impressed
laborers uttered sighs of admiration
nobody talked nonsense any more
(though more surprises arose later)

The dismantling progressed smoothly
great-great-grandchildren putting their hands
on great-great-grandfathers' fingerprints
(about 130 years after their time)
The dismantling progressed smoothly
in the reverse order of construction

## VII.  Fort

Hurry, before the rain stops
Keep working until dawn comes
villagers are moving stones
women and children, mothers too with babies
          on their backs
carry stone
soaking wet under torch light

They have no time to size the stone
for the enemy attack may begin tomorrow
men pile blocks of stone
from the roadside and beaches
But the method is far from random
under the dim torch light
stone blocks are connected tightly
and a fort is near completion
on top of the seaside hill
so that it will turn back arrows and bullets

Here in the coastal region of Southern Ireland
is a village that has a history of fighting
Vikings' attacks and Anglo-Saxon invasions
located near the monumental grave of New Grange
said to be erected in 3,000 B. C.
Not for power
Neither for formation of aesthetic legacies
nor for show of forces

but for the protection of villagers
for the honor of ancestors killed in battle
      against pirates and invaders
for the unification of the Celts
they must fight
entrenched in the fort everyone helped build
they take up the challenge
until they succeed
protecting lives, families, farmlands, and love
In the grass at the bottom of the hill
are scattered old tombstones
  --Johan Mhara, 40, and son John, 16
   on July 7, 1578
   fought here and killed
The name Mhara is Irish and means sea
appropriate for those who loved the sea
as brave fisherman father and son
(Quite a few Mhara now remain around here
  open a telephone directory, for instance
  many Irish names contain Hara
  such as O'Hara, Bhara, and Mhara)
Villagers made on the tombstones
inscriptions of love
after they had repelled the enemy
The darkened stone of the fort's walls
has thus withstood 500, even 1,000 years
For they contain iron?
Iron ties and stone's union
as tight as the Celts
must have added durability to the walls

The pebbles carried by children and their mothers
fill the gaps
in the stone blocks that men carried
and weeds cover the bottom of the walls

Great-great-grandfather had no way of knowing
today's travelers do not notice
that a history of stone lives on
the Irish language that the villagers speak
will die out sooner
only English is understood in town now
tide of water eroding old inlets

## VIII.  Softness

Sea water reaches here as the tide rises
and the reeds are mud-stained
Mud may be all around the Eyeglasses Bridge
but the surrounding area is actually sandy
only the base of the girder
the stone pillar that forms the arches
was found to be mud-filled
Why is only that part of the land soft
what can account for it?
Yûzô Yamaguchi kept asking
isn't the foundation of any bridge supposed
      to be gravel
or solid rock?
(all other bridges in the area were so, even the ones
  downstream had no mud in the foundations)
How strange it is that the most critical part of
      the bridge
where 40 tons per square meter concentrate
is filled with a large quantity of gray *tôfu*-like stuff!
Under the water the bottom is like cottage cheese
on which pine ties are laid
and then slabs
large stone blocks on top of them--
The structure is softest at the bottom

How can it be explained?
in the dark cottage cheese-like mud

52 of them in all
each 15 centimeters in diameter, a little over
     one meter long
the pointed posts looked like they were laid yesterday
floating straight in the cottage cheese
without even touching bottom

Yûzô Yamaguchi was speechless
how bold and daring the great-great-grandfathers'
     dynamics were
how insolent their modesty!
Solid evidence of their mastery of softness
that challenges modern bridge construction
If earthquake occures, the bridge sways
and returns precisely to the original position
The ties, the mud, and the posts
are to absorb the enormous weight
rather than to resist it
the posts' ends just touching bottom
in the basin of mud

Yûzô Yamaguchi took it to his heart
the deepest secret of the bridge
that endured the numerous floods
as though nothing ever happened

--Come to think of it, I felt something was different
  I mean my feet could feel the stone
  It was soft
  like the snow that bounces back from the soles
     of your feet

I suppose it's the same principle as the
railroad ties that serve as springs

That's it
I never thought that was hard stone--
An old laborer puffed cigarette smoke and said
--Hey, you talk like a poet
Young laborers teased him
--You mean the bridge actually moved?
--Have you ever seen a suspension bridge
made of stone?

--Be serious, men
I've crossed this bridge many times since I was a boy
and I felt the same every time I crossed it
even after this dismantling began
my soles felt the bridge swaying
--Like Columbus's egg, hah
--Your legs were shaking, man
--You may be getting a stroke soon!
the young men mock
the old man falls silent
(It's true that wearing wooden clogs on the bridge
feel like straw sandals)

## IX.  LISBOA


*Here in Nagasaki we have no trouble walking*
*around even on rainy days, wearing wooden clogs . . .*
Great-great-grandfathers wrote home from Nagasaki
The scientist Gen'nai Hiraga wrote so too
referring to Nagasaki's cobblestones
that shed rain water to the gutters to flow away

Young Great-great-grandfather in the Portugal he
      had dreamed of
asks the way of an old man in Lisbon
The old man asks something back and says
Go straight up the hill
His hand, like his chin, points the direction
Great-great-grandfather thanks him and gets excited
for the hill is almost like Nagasaki's
He looks back
the old Portuguese man is also climbing
the narrow cobblestone slope
quietly like the fado that leaks from the eaves
Beyond the old man, in the distant harbor
is a slim, long bridge elegantly stretching
an aqueduct built more than 100 years ago
Great-great-grandfather came here
to  Lisbon of the seven hills
to see the aqueduct
and to sketch the bridge from a distance
      with a Japanese brush

It's important to feel the bridge with your own hands
and learn stone's union
but you must also examine the bridge from a distance
and learn of its beauty in the setting
Look at the bridge from underneath
and find the beauty behind things
the aesthetics that holds up the sky--
so taught a Dutch bridge builder to Great-
      great-grandfather
That's what he came to Lisbon for
on his way back from Rotterdam

Great-great-grandfather had seen over 1,000 bridges
      in Amsterdam
the stone bridges in the city of water and canals
However, Amsterdam had no hills
and Great-great-grandfather from Nagasaki
      was left with questions
Observation of bridges in a flat city had limitations
so Great-great-grandfather went boating
      through the canals
and saw the beauty of the undersides varying
      with each bridge
Reflections of the bridges trembled
in water under Holland's blue sky
and Holland taught him bridges' beauty, technique,
      and function
He learned circumferential geometry applied
      to the bridges
and he mastered the calculation of the ratio
(but the figures are good only in Holland where
  there are neither mountains, hills, typhoons,
  nor floods)

Now in Lisbon, standing on a hill, he comes
    to understand
(the beautiful and strong bridge must withstand
 sea winds, storms, earthquakes, and floods)
Pulling up the trousers which he was beginning
    to get used to
in the breeze from Lisbon's sea
Great-great-grandfather's youthful dreams
    continued to grow

The hill that Great-great-grandfather climbed
must have been one of the many mazelike roads
    in old Alfama
On top of it stands St. George's Castle
where perhaps Great-great-grandfather was going
Feeling his shoulder touch
a Portuguese who came down the slope
Great-great-grandfather must have been stricken
    by nostalgia
as he looked back to see Europe's longest bridge
suspended over the Tejo River
and the sun setting beyond it
the Castle's stone staircase reflects the yellowish light

At Lisbon he soon got on a sailing boat
loaded with goods for Nagasaki
with confeitos and pão de Castella
(It is presumed that the pão
 gathered mold and hardened like stone
 during the more than five-month-long journey)

It has long been believed
that Japanese stone bridges used Chinese technology

But Great-great-grandfather's footsteps indicate
that a direct route existed to carry European bridge
        contruction techniques to Nagasaki
across the great seas
(travelling slowly through what Great-great-
  grandfather called the sky above the sea's bottom)
In other words
as important as the Silk Road that ran through China
there was a sea route
and the same technique was brought into Japan
        via both routes

The old man who pointed his chin skyward in Lisbon
and showed Great-great-grandfather the way
would probably have continued his ascent
crossing sky's bridge, into the distant clouds
Great-great-grandfathers followed him
in heaven if you meet them
and ask them the way
they would surely point their chins downward
toward the earth, to the port of Lisbon
and speak in the old familiar seaman's voice
--Go straight down the hill
Exactly as told
many lives went down to the sea
passing the flooded Eyeglasses Bridge
like tiny trout
Stone, the stone bridge, persists
letting time flow incessantly

## X.   Human Sacrifice


Soon the tide will rise
like treasure hunters
laborers poke carefully around the foundation
with sticks
some use brushes to clear the gaps
They are looking for bones, or chips
for they have believed since their childhood
that humans were sacrificed at the Eyeglasses Bridge
No one doubted it
even before the dismantling began
all expected to find their beliefs confirmed
Fortunately for them the water receded
should human bones be washed downstream
they'll be discovered in water

Yet no bones were found
not even a chip
One worker found a fresh cat skull
and got excited
--It still has some hair on it

At the lowest layer of the pile
were two slabs of stone which had holes
60 cm in diameter, 24 cm deep
in the shape of milling stones
Some speculated that the holes were for
          sacrificial bones
but would they have done that
at a time when bodies were buried?

Suppose the modern interpretation were valid
there should at least be a few bones in the holes
But there was no trace of bones, just some sand
--Look, these are women's parts
For that matter
pictures of human intercourse had been found
      engraved
on the back of slabs in the upper layer
There were also coarse carvings of lotus flowers
and commanding warriors on horseback
Such reliefs are not uncommon
routinely found in stone structures throughout
      the world
Graffiti in a shadowy place
stonemasons' pastime, their prayer, or their spite
together with sculptures of all sorts
are said to abound on the backs of stones
of the 4,000 year-old pyramids
(the significance of the holes was not determined
      in the end)

--What a disappointment
as the laborers' lament testifies
the legend is merely a legend
This is just pure functionalism
a show of the great-great-grandfathers' cynicism
In the depth of the dry, spring sky
their laughter resounds
like explosions of fireworks

## XI.  SON ET LUMIÈRE

Fireworks are shot overhead
all the lights are off
the live music
suddenly stops
Explosions of fireworks!
The summer castle festival in the Loire Valley
a symphony of *son et lumière*
a series of *services* that the castles offer to tourists
The tour guide who lectured on the castles' history
          during the day
is asleep in a chair
The fireworks are interspersed with music

Here by the River Loire
over 100 castles and mansions remain
From a time like Japan's Muromachi to
          Azuchi-Momoyama periods, or maybe
          the beginning of the Edo period
Strong men fought everywhere and left with us
          a legacy of history's rise and fall
The legacy is made of stone
in the middle reaches of France's longest river, the Loire
fertile land, mild climate, grain and wine
gorgeous women and intrigues
faith, murder, bribes
and scars of swords and bullets
on stone steps, balconies and walls
on the fireplaces

Tourists touch them
and they shine with grime
(an intersecton of history and man!)
The cobblestones that once bounced back
      the wheels
of elegant horse-drawn carriages lie cool
fabulous gardens and noblemen's rooms
--Where was the kitchen and where the stoves
--What about the bath and laundry rooms?
      Where did they dry diapers?
--Where were the maids' and servants' quarters?
The guide is at a loss for answers
to questions from these tourists, obviously
      housewives
Official history seems to eclipse these things
--Well, you see, the river
  the river flooded and washed them away
  though there were a lot of them, I'm sure
The Loire Valley basked in the summer sun
hazy reflection of light from the river below

Upstream on the Chang-ching River
the stone tower at Chungking
casts a shadow in the fertile Szechwan Basin
The walls are simple
and were never stained with blood
This tower observed in silence
the stream of events in the vastness below
News from the Chungking branch
in a Chinese paper of Aug. 9, 1984 read:

*RESTORATION OF CHUNGKING STONE TOWER*
*--The oldest extant stone tower in Chungking, the*
*tower which has serenely looked over the northern*
*reach of the river since the Sung Dynasty, was*
*completely renovated in July and now is open to the*
*public. Originally built in 1167 as a square-*
*shaped, seven story, 35 m high pagoda, it used*
*quality-cut stone and no iron, nails, nor wood.*
*Buddhist images are carved on the sides of each story.*
*The tower has now come to life.*

But there too
tourists must be swarming
--How beautiful!  Sublime!
uttering such words
The guidebook must contain the same information
in the same wording as in the paper
But no artificial *son et lumière* will be there
only the color of nature will be
If they did not use iron or wood
they wouldn't have used a bit of cement
The restoration workers probably wanted
         to use cement
but 800 years of history kept them from using it
That's the golden rule of restoration
for all historical buildings

What is restoration
or reconstruction?
What on earth is preservation?

## XII.  Reconstruction

To preserve is to maintain
the present condition
What once existed in its own right
becomes what needs to be protected
From what was functioning to what
        needs protection--
a degeneration of purpose
Preservation's tense is the past
or the present perfect
because what is protected is compressed "present"
which is already in the past
In Aristotle's rhetoric
it's the historical present for visualizing
        the past
In Buddhism
it's the presence of illusory matter
or the art of presenting the past
(Words like ecology and environment are
        today's clichés
  but using nature for man's convenience is not natural
  it's man's conceit or nature's degeneration
  or man's degeneration
  Fashionable words smell like a hospital)
--What is preserved must not be altered
--The original state should not be changed
seem to represent the protectionists' views
which are auspicious laws of the land

Man's wisdom to continue only in the past tense
what has stopped functioning
or ceased influencing
calling it preservation
like the Egyptian mummies

Restoration thus means
to remove the conditions that prevent fulfillment
        of the function
and reconstruction
is to revive what's perished and preserve it
But often what's reconstructed is kept from functioning
for fear of damage
If it's a bridge, crossing is
if a house, living is prohibited
their functions reduced to the minimum
Some even charge admission
an economic vice
calculated to repay the cost and still preserve
(we gracefully pay money
  for protected "nature"
  without questioning if nature could charge money)

To repeat
reconstruction is more negative than preservation
double-sealing of what's past
*imitation* or copy

Yûzô Yamaguchi, devoted to recontruct the
        Eyeglasses Bridge
exhausted himself day and night

There were gaps in the arch's stone blocks
yet he wasn't allowed even to shave them
he was to reproduce the original bridge
(That was the order of the Cultural Agency
  now it is the matter of his pride)
knowing that the work is more difficult than
            rewriting
a manuscript destroyed in fire
for stone blocks are emphatically there
it's definitely more difficult than dismantling
Yûzô Yamaguchi measured every stone
2,800 pieces in all
precisely, down to millimeters
and recorded them over several months
He went to the stonemasons' union
to have all the pieces made 1/5 the actual size

Reduced-size stone blocks were made
(amid the stonemasons' complaints and gripes)
then a pair of scaffolds for the arch, in reduced scale
to produce a model, a mini-copy of the bridge
10 meters long and 1.7 meters high
was made and remade
calculations and experiments were done and redone
Yûzô Yamaguchi's records show how he worked
but no one but him really knows how much he
            exerted himself
The great success of the reconstruction of the bridge
was solely due to the careful experiments
The Eyeglasses Bridge was reconstructed two years after
            it was dismantled
in a pond in a nearby park

There is a record by Yûzô Yamaguchi
that the bridge made an ominous noise
as the final stone block was fit in at the arch's top
and the supports were removed
Yûzô Yamaguchi heard the noise
of the gaps narrowing and the stone tightening
the bridge functioning
the noise getting louder
when laborers, afraid the bridge might collapse
ran from beneath the arches
--It's all right, I'm right here with you
he shouted to calm the laborers

Reconstruction was done
the designated national cultural property
        was built again
Yûzô Yamaguchi's efforts were commendable
his passion for reconstruction
will be remembered for a long time
the Eyeglasses Bridge looks beautiful
elegant yet magnificent
However, no flood can test this reconstructed bridge
there will be no chance for this bridge to hold
        itself in perfect balance
Built by modern dynamics, using wooden
        trusses and jacks
this bridge might well be sturdier
than the one built with the great-great-
        grandfathers' sandbag method
Those who opposed reconstruction
would not dare oppose protection of the
        reconstructed bridge

which has neither fence nor admission booth
the bridge doesn't have farmers and townspeople
     who cross it
(children too do not come to this cultural property
 so a legend of human sacrifice will not be created)
the bridge simply lies there still
The Eyeglasses Bridge, stand there
forever . . .
as Yûzô Yamaguchi prayed
the bridge will endure
But irrelevant to his efforts and prayers
the fact remains
that the reconstructed bridge is a copy
an object to recollect the past
a sample of the beautiful "historical present"
The "original" reconstructed bridge that casts its shadow
on the murky water is in the past tense

## XIII.  Gaudí


Not to let the present pass
not to put an end to existence or time
one could continue tenaciously
construction for milleniums
like La Sagrada Familia Church in Barcelona, Spain
like Antonio Gaudí's work now popular in Japan
Some say the work depended on poor
        people's contributions
so it will take another 100 years to complete
which is probably true
Whatever, the fact is
that in nearly 100 years after its inception in 1882
only one or two fifths of the work is finished
Suppose another 100 years are needed
it is a 200-year present progressive tense
Do the hasty Japanese really like such duration?
they noisily talk about Gaudí at every occasion
(Slow progress is common in Europe
  the Notre Dame at Rouen, Normandy, France
  was started in 1201
  and completed in 1530
  spanning 330 years
  the fabulous cathedral that Monet so loved to paint
  the right steeple called Tour de Brou
  the left one Tour de Saint-Romain
  enticing beauties melting into Normandy's sky
  the butterlike color of the stone
  is said to be because the cathedral was financed
  by profits from the region's butter . . .)

Gaudí is just fine
Dalí, from the same town as Gaudí, proclaimed
that architecture was for artists to make a living
Children play in a park Gaudí built
piling natural rocks from Spanish fields
playhouses shaped like cylinders, cycads,
stone caves, palm trees, mushrooms, and sunflowers
corn cobs, cockscombs, and onions
lotus flowers and Buddha heads
ah how fanciful they are
absorbing children
these are adult's playthings
innocent mosaics of stone
not so outrageous but unique in shape and color
the joy of play
This rhythm is manifested in the pattern
the pattern is given life by the rhythm
like the flow of prose without punctuation
or verse that uses punctuation marks
He does not hesitate over anything
so he even uses cement freely

It is all right therefore to go along with Gaudí
like a certain Japanese architect building
      a tower in Osaka
stealing Gaudí's ideas
Critics praise Gaudí and make a living
but they ignore the playing children
and make only journalistic commentaries
(though being sensational could also be playful)

The name Gaudí stands out in the sky
(though in Japan it will be a temporary phenomenon)
(how could it last for 20 years, let alone 200?)
(perhaps no more than two years?)

Suppose you build brilliant towers and houses
            next to Gaudí's
would Gaudí's authenticity be blemished?
What's hurt would be the pride of those "individualists"
            who worship authority
Ironically, it is they who are hurting Gaudí
looking down on children playing in Gaudí Park
uttering words of praise, showing off
under the bright sun of Spain
(like at the Notre Dame of Paris where mass has
            degenerated to a show)
which is irrelevant to Gaudí (to Christianity too)
They always praise individuality
it's the myth of individualism, heroism, and genius!
Notice some parts of Gaudí's tower crumbling as it's built
or its pink shell color slowly fading!
(unless you climb it step by step
  feeling it with the soles of your feet
  unless you reach the 100 meter tower's top
  and touch by hand the protruding ornaments
  or closely examine the wine-color and
            cobalt-blue mosaic tiles
  you'll probably never notice it)

Fifty years from now
more damage will show
but don't worry, advocates of Gaudí

you can just repair them
for it will still be under construction anyway
Repair work on something which is still
          under construction!
it will be different from ordinary repairs
It will be like touch-up or adjustments
(in poetry, it's revision)
a present progressive form without an end

The Notre Dame of Rouen that took 330 years
          to complete
shows subtle variations of Gothic style
reflecting changes in taste
and design in those three hundred years
(it also proves that no single man was responsible
          for the design)
The variations render a marvelous depth to Notre Dame
(the softness of the material made the variations possible)
Great-great-grandfather had learned how hard the stone
          in Europe was
and realized how soft-textured Japanese stone was
If he had seen this cathedral in Rouen
or limestone in Normandy
he would have gained confidence and intimacy
The countless number of holes in the walls
created by the German army's mortar shells and bullets
show how soft Normandy's stone is
(cold  physics can measure
  stone's hardness by the bullet holes
  still remaining in European cities
  but it cannot compare them, for example
  with those in the Loire castles

or in the buildings of Alsace since the Spanish-
      French War
We need research on the history of cannons)


--You ask me about Gaudí?
he is a great artisan
like Picasso, Dalí, Casals
and Miró who by the way is from the same town
they are a bunch of artisans
Monsieur Brunet the stone furniture maker
the artist from Paris' 12th District is critical
His comments are not necessarily far-fetched
in fact, his is more clear-cut than Parisian
      intellectuals'
who, smiling cynically
(sipping cognac)
would say that Gaudí is passé
that they dislike Gaudí's rustic style
even though they are profiting from his popularity
Blasé Paris critics seem uninterested in Gaudí
nor do they seem interested in the opinion
of the Japanese who stammers on about stone
You can imagine
how Westerners treated Great-great-grandfather
who, with a gleam in his eyes
traveled to Europe to study stone


Monsieur Brunet is completely taken in by the *jizô*
--You are absolutely right
suppose we build a building named Audi
(he does not even grin
 Audi is a German car very popular in Paris)

just next to the Gaudí Park
the Catalonians will not be happy
(the Catalonians are the people of Catalonia
      whose capital was Barcelona)
they will quickly destroy it
Would the Japanese destroy a roadside *jizô*
if someone built a new one next to it?
No one would think that the old *jizô* was blemished
Your pictures showed me
many different *jizô* co-existing in one place
statues made by nameless people, not by any
      one artist
grouped together in one place
A *jizô* standing alone looks good
but many *jizô* standing around at random
      are superb
(because not one of them is insisting on
      individuality)
Why don't the Japanese study *jizô*
instead of coming all the way to Barcelona?
I'm not saying that you shouldn't have come
but I just don't understand

--You say if an individual artist blends into
      a town and brings joy to the town, he's good?
you're right
that's great individualistic art
but Gaudí applies his talent to subjugate stone
      and mosaic
That's where *jizô* differs
Yes, he makes use of stone at his will
whereas *jizô* . . . (he's so obsessed by *jizô*)

in *jizô*, nameless artists follow stone's will
giving life to stone
without a bit of unnaturalness
rather modestly
that's why *jizô* is usually anonymous
Gaudí is not so
he always shows off his name
Picasso, Dalí, and Miró
may not show off their names themselves
but others do it for them
for them the names are important
That's the difference

## XIV.  Stoneship


Monsieur Brunet begins to look like one of the
     great-great-grandfathers
The great-great-grandfathers learned from the West
but never forgot Japan
Those who were taken in by the West were
     later generations
great-grandfathers downward
the young people from the Meiji period
(when the generation gap was not a concern)
The great-great-grandfathers wore a topknot
two swords on the belt
and a kimono with a family's crest, *hakama,*
     and white socks
81 of them, samurai led by the Lord of Buzen
sailed to America
and demonstrated their dignity
It was during the first year of Man'en (1860)
Walt Whitman wrote a long passage
praising them in the *Leaves of Grass*
(the poem called "A Broadway Pageant")
Not only the samurai
but the great-great-grandfathers before then
merchants and engineers
went out to Europe or America
What they learned and how they did
are recorded in books and documents
so they need not be mentioned

Only they never felt they were inferior
because their world was so different
they brought back all they learned
weaving, wine-making, printing, bridge
      construction, and glass-blowing
Our Great-great-grandfather was one of them
but he was interested only in one thing:
      bridge construction
the technique of piling stone blocks
how to connect stone to stone, how to arch,
      how to use wedges, cutters, and levers
More essential was the circumferential ratio
he calculated it with a small abacus he brought
      from Japan
mastered how to figure out curves and inclines
and the specific gravity therein
He recorded them on a notebook hand-made in Japan
with a Japanese brush and ink he carried in a pouch
(Ascertaining the accuracy of the Japanese higher
      mathematics he studied in Nagasaki
  and finding that trigonometry and circumference in
      old Japan used the same principles as in the West
  he marveled many times
  at the genius of the pioneer mathematicians, Takakazu
      Seki and his students)


Straight lines, curves, and tight joints
reduction of resistance
and above all flexibility--
Doesn't bridge construction resemble ship building?

The year-long sea voyage of Great-great-
      grandfather's time
was dangerous, but a precious learning experience
He learned conversation
(the crews were full of language teachers)
and the writing system in ink and brush
But the greatest event of note
occurred on his way back
Great-great-grandfather was shocked to notice
why didn't he realize it earlier
that the movement of the ship
the constant repetition of rocking and pitching
is like an earthquake, in slow tempo
the ship recovers from a tilt
lets the waves roll under
and returns precisely to the original position
This restoring power!
at the time of a tsunami or flood--

Great-great-grandfather could not sleep
      in excitement
like a school kid who solved a difficult problem
he was elated
--That's it, a stoneship!
The keel supporting the great weight of stone
and the sea underneath it!
(European bridges are all on solid foundations
  their data on the use of gravel and the layout
      of foundations
  all laboriously copied
  But those bridges will not withstand earthquakes
      in Japan

they haven't considered typhoons or floods
nor the weakness of solid foundations
They have not taken the sea into consideration)
Great-great-grandfather had written--
*Ballast . . . pronounced "barasuto" or "barasu"*
*gravel laid at the foundation of a building, but*
  *originally in ship's bottoms for the purpose of*
  *balancing and stabilizing the ship*
*if more barasuto less sway? not necessarily, the*
  *weight of the ship and its load, their total and their*
  *locations must be realistically considered; there's also*
  *a need to calculate the "energy" of the waves applied*
  *to the ship, in addition a need to compare the data*
  *with that gained when the ship was empty*
Great-great-grandfather continued his study on the ship
the captain and the crew were surprised by questions
--Since when did you want to become a seaman?
Great-great-grandfather, raised in Nagasaki,
        was unaffected by the ship's motion
uttered "Let's go, Stoneship!"

## XV.   Singularity of Style


Monsieur Brunet wants to go by boat
his wife sides with this idea
Brunet is infatuated by *jizô*
after seeing them in 10 or so pictures
he insists on saving money to go to Japan
Having learned that only a Polish freighter
            takes passengers
and that the fare is high
(2,000 US dollars per person
  20,000 in the weakening franc
  about 500,000 yen in Japan)
as much as 40,000 francs for two
(actually two times that for a round trip)
Brunet raises his arms
spreads them four times as wide as his shoulders
cried out, "Que le diable t'emporte!"
How can a socialist charge such a high tariff?
The impetuous wife agrees
--Let's quit
--Going by boat?
--Non, going to japon; the pictures are enough
The wife's opinion may be a good one
they may be better off not going to Japan
where today cement *jizô* are sold
highways are built all over
and the roadside *jizô* are gone
only to be sold by antiquarians at exorbitant prices
Besides, not all *jizô* are worthwhile to see

smooth-faced dolls made with electric chisels
are good for nothing
Even if Brunet comes to Japan and raises his voice
     in protest
it will be too late
If, as Monsieur Allado once said
the cobblestone were a remnant of buggy roads
the *jizô* could be called a remnant of old
     straw-sandal roads
(there is no sign that they are "protected")
If it is a remnant
*jizô* has lost its *style* that is alive
while the cobblestone in Paris is still alive
withstanding the enormous traffic
(see by yourself from the sidewalk)
heaving and bouncing back from the cars

What gave life to *jizô*'s style
was neither *jizô* nor stone
It was the times, or the people of that period
that included the artist
Even if the *jizô* remains, it's only in form
*jizô*'s style is dead

It will never revive
Yet Brunet is moved by it
that is not because of his taste for the old
but because of his ability
to suddenly become a contemporary of another time
of the great-great-grandfathers, great-grandfathers,
     and grandfathers
an interesting phenomenon

Both the function and beauty of *jizô* are gone
today's love for *jizô* is what is called curiosity
to bring back the past through symbols and pictures
Brunet's case is close to it
*Jizô*'s style diminished little by little
the people of the straw sandal age took it
       to another world
today thieves carry away what's left in cars

Singularity of style
means something lives just for the time of its life
Once vibrant style
can never re-live the same life
(curiosity seekers and researchers are
       professional mediums?)
The Japanese have lost the kind of life that gave
       life to *jizô*
they no longer possess critical eyes

## XVI.  Eyeglasses


--Grandpa, your eyes are dead, you can't see it
an innocent remark only close relatives may make
An old man led by a young girl stands on the bridge
holding a cane and stretching his back
he tries to see but gives up
--You say I won't?
the old man kids
There are lots of spectators on the bridge

They came to see every day
the stone bridge looking like a pair of eyeglasses
            with its reflection on water
at the time few people had ever seen eyeglasses
what "eyeglasses" were was completely unknown
They saw the fascinating pattern of reflections
rather than the bridge itself

Eyeglasses were brought to Japan in 1616
the second year of Gan'en at the beginning
            of the Edo period
(Chinese characters were adopted and
            pronounced *megane*)
There is a record
that 23 dozen eyeglasses were imported through
            a British firm in Hirado
(Predating this, two pairs of eyeglasses, large and small
   believed to have belonged to Shôgun Ieyasu, exist
            at Ieyasu's shrine, Tôshôgû

no doubt a tribute from a foreign country
There is also a theory that earlier than that around 1550
a pair was brought to Japan by Indians
Still earlier in 1539 St. Francis Xavier brought one
and gave it to the Lord of Suô, Yoshitaka Ôuchi
so records but no evidence exist
If substantiated, it will be an exceptional case)
But who bought the 23 dozen eyeglasses that came
       to Hirado?
they must have been enormously expensive
irrelevant to people's lives

The birth of Japanese eyeglasses
like so many other objects of civilization
took place in Nagasaki
The year was 1624 (the first year of Kan'ei)
when glass was polished to produce lenses
but an eyeglasses store didn't open until several
       decades later
Even then it was irrelevant to ordinary people
Grand Councilor Hikozaemon Ôkubo and men
       of his class might have used them

A strange object named Eyeglasses Bridge was
       built with stone
over the River Nakashima in Nagasaki
in 1634 (the eleventh year of Kan'ei)
10 years after eyeglasses were made
Curious people, all dressed up, came to Nagasaki
from neighboring towns, fishing villages, and farm lands
crossing mountains and valleys

Many carried rolled mats and cushions diagonally
      on their backs
lunches on their belts
The rich brought stacks of lacquered lunch boxes
and flocked in Nagasaki
--what is *megane*?
--glass balls that you see things through
--in that case, if you go to Eyeglasses Bridge
      you can see better?
--no, you can't
--what are eyeglasses anyway?
Two arches and their reflections on the river's surface
indeed look like a pair of eyes
The water is glistening like glass
Near-sighted, far-sighted, weak-sighted, blind,
      diseased eyes all gathered on this side,
      the other side, and on the bridge
--can you see? can you?
--no, I can't see nothing
No one can laugh at such people
(for it was as recent as the beginning of the twentieth
      century
  that a mother, hearing that a wire would send goods
      to her son
  hung a parcel on an electric pole in the Japanese
      countryside)

Just for the record . . .
Old stone bridges called Eyeglasses Bridge--
      regardless of how the words were written--
      numbered 342 in Japan
of which 131 were destroyed and 210 remain
"old" means only up to the end of the Edo period

the majority of them are in Kyûshû
clustering in Nagasaki, Kumamoto, and
      Fukuoka prefectures
the oldest being Nagasaki's
seven are designated as Cultural Treasure
but the most grandiose and elegant is Isahaya's
      Eyeglasses Bridge
known for its 50 meter span and large blocks of stone
the one Yûzô Yamaguchi worked on

The origin of the bridge tells
how the Eyeglasses Bridge was innovative at the time
how a nameless young man burned with passion
      and exertion
how Great-great-grandfather was involved in it
(Great-great-grandfather's baggage, returning
      to Nagasaki
 is likely to have contained
 several pairs of Dutch eyeglasses)
Historical documents indicate
that Nagasaki's Eyeglasses Bridge used the Chinese
      monk Ju-ting's techniques
(this is mentioned again and again)
though Ju-ting may have rendered help and instructions
Great-great-grandfather's contribution should
      never be discounted
without him there would have been no bridges

It was not only the newness of the *megane* bridge
nor was it the rarity of the shape
but people crossed it lovingly

The bridge was beneficial, sturdy, and beautiful
(the town would be safe even if the river flooded)
some people bowed to it before crossing it
What makes a bridge a bridge is people's feet
not material and technology
The feet of the people who cross it make it beautiful
creating the Eyeglasses Bridge's style
a literary style in solid stone
People loved the bridge
as proud of it as of their homeland
And the bridge grew with them

## XVII.   Stone and Language


Something grows after a thing is made
as a bridge grows after being built
The end of a work is its beginning
Completion is only an impetus
but for all these
the first *thing* must be prepared solidly
the *thing* appropriate for new growth
in accordance with reason . . .
If it's a bridge, the foundation
the connection of stone with stone
the distribution of the force of gravity
and most of all, humility . . .
(does humility only refer to a quality of mind?
  it shouldn't)

Once many stone bridges were built
and many were lost
some were demolished for fear of collapse
a few collapsed by themselves in the course
            of construction
no doubt as a result of the laborers'
            over-reliance on experience
or over-confidence on themselves or on stone
The life of a bridge depends on how relaxed
            their minds were
humility is the absence of relaxation
it is the act of listening to stone and following it
with no arbitrariness

(only then, the ultimate bridge will arch from
    its original site)


*The loneliness of Bashô who slept with a stone*
*and sang in the field; that doesn't work today*
wrote Tekkan Yosano
(what Tekkan really meant is hard to know)
Bashô probably sought stone's severity in language
nothing is as free and flexible as language
(Tekkan must have wanted at that time
  to use language vividly, like fire)
The resemblance and conflicts
between language and stone


Yet Bashô wrote poetry
by questioning language
by rolling it one thousand times on his tongue--
like the stonemasons in Paris
picking the exact piece of stone
to lay next to stone
(measuring and weighing one by one
  the shape, size, weight, and ridgeline of the
      granite stone)
Bashô was never arbitrary
(and built an ultimate bridge connecting heart
    and matter)


If Brunet found Bashô
he would say emphatically
--Yes, Bashô is almost like *jizô*, more so than Gaudí

But today
cement is poured
for building modern bridges
or to produce *jizô* to sell
decorated *jizô*
with large price tags
charismatic *jizô* with egoistic "I" from tip to toe
acrobatic *jizô* making faces
tormenting *jizô* doing headstands
bearded *jizô* with a grin
*jizô* wearing sunglasses
*jizô* that contain music boxes in the stomachs
These *jizô* are dressed up by the store owner
with red bibs and loin cloths

How lucky Molière was!
he wrote plays
like a laborer dug sewers
or a craftsman assembled table parts--
so remarked Allan
(Allan was praising modesty
and the artist who learns from the material)
a remark one would want to dedicate to Brunet

It has been a long time since language was used
        as casually as fire, clay, or cement
it's as though people believed language would
        obey the heart
and be manipulated as the heart wished--
Language became a river rather than stone
to flow beneath the bridge and cause a flood
(the Buddhist river of No Return)

So separate language from the heart
let it loose in the field again
move it at least to the other side of the river
(leaving the heart on this side)

Then dream
of an eternal bridge built with the stones
of language which were cut
and carried out one by one
The magnificant Eyeglasses Bridge
        of language
that rests its foundation on your
        flexible thought!

As I row out to the flowing river and
        look up
the arch extending to the sky
the underside of the language shines
on rippling water
it's soon weatherbeaten
enduring earthquakes and floods
        gently swaying
communicating with many hearts
and watching the river flow
the Eyeglasses Bridge continues to grow!

## Afterword
### --a personal expression--

The theme of this long poem is something I nurtured for over twenty years. I once considered presenting it in the form of an essay or novel, but I finally decided to use verse. While writing it, I thought the choice was appropriate. I still think so.

In the flood depicted in Section II, I lost a very dear friend, who had understood my writings and selflessly supported me even if we lived far apart. This friend went to rescue someone drowning in flood water, and he never returned alive. His death was the most shocking event of my youth. The war had ended and we were celebrating that we would not lose any more lives, just when his painful death asaulted me.

However, I entirely excluded my personal feelings from this work. I was determined not to use even the first person pronoun "I" in it. As a result, my desire to dedicate this work to the deceased friend grew stronger.

The great-great-grandfather that frequently appears in the work is a fictional persona, but a man who might really have existed. I have included in the work reasons for saying this. The existence of Great-great-grandfather was crucial for the work.

Other personae are real, or they are people who actually lived, though I have changed their names in some cases. Among them, to Mr. Yûzô Yamaguchi, whose real name I used, I would like to express both my gratitude and apology at this time. My work owes much to his book called *Kyûshû no ishibashi o tazunete* (Homage to the Stone Bridges in Kyûshû), 3 v., Shôwadô, 1975-76. Without his book and his technical research my work would have become quite a different piece, losing much of its substance. I thank him from the bottom of my heart and at the same time I renew my admiration for his great achievements. If I can be even more personal here, I would like to make an announcement that a few years ago, at my aunt's funeral, I learned that Yûzô Yamaguchi was related to my family. I was surprised, and felt that what I had considered just a poetic theme became closer to me.

Last year, in the spring of 1984, I got on a freighter of foreign nationality and left Yokohama to go to the Netherlands. In a cabin of the boat, I began preparations for this poem, thinking that there would be no other time to put my long-kept theme to writing. However, I could not begin writing it until later, when I stayed in Paris for about a year. I completed the first draft during the stay, though I had study to do and functions to perform. Seldom did I feel that it was a peripheral activity, however. Most of the time, I was convinced that writing was my most important work. Even on my return trip to Japan via America I always had a notebook full of manuscripts and worked on them whether on plane or train, every night until late, absent-mindedly neglecting business or friends. This book results from those memorable experiences.

Some readers might regard this as a book of tourism. It is true that it contains many scenes I actually saw or heard about during my visit to Europe both this time and more than ten years ago. That does not particularly bother me. The main part of what I had nurtured as my theme could not possibly have been treated in any other way. This is to say that my mind is now in an egocentric state of both satisfaction and resignation.

I also have a certain degree of insolence that makes me say that it is too late for me to do anything about the work's polish or techniques. In fact, I was hard put trying to downscale the work from some three thousand lines to about two thousand. During this lull before both favorable and unfavorable criticism will surely be handed to me, I am content with the result and feel that I was able to clear my debts to life.

My thanks are due to Mr. Yasuo Shimizu of Seidosha who agreed to publish such a selfish work as this. I also thank Ms. Junko Takahashi of the Editorial Department for assistance.

The cover design was prepared, as in my previous books, by Mr. Mitsuru Hirano.

Shirô Hara
July, 1985

# CORNELL UNIVERSITY EAST ASIA PAPERS

For information on ordering the preceding publications
and tapes, please write to:

EAST ASIA PAPERS
East Asia Program
Cornell University
140 Uris Hall
Ithaca, NY   14853-7601

Milton Keynes UK
Ingram Content Group UK Ltd.
UKHW012104280923
429583UK00002B/228